My Book of
WISDOM

By Oluchi O. Nnadi

Copyright © 2024 Oluchi O. Nnadi. All rights reserved.
First paperback edition printed 2016
ISBN 978-1-913455-69-9
No part of this book shall be reproduced or transmitted in any form or by any means,
electronic or mechanical, including photocopying, recording, or by any information retrieval
system without written permission of the publisher.
Published by Scribblecity Publications
Printed in Great Britain

Although every precaution has been taken in the preparation of this book, the publisher and
author assume no responsibility for errors or omissions. Neither is any liability assumed for
damages resulting from the use of this information contained herein.

Dedicated to

The Almighty God. To Chiazokam, Chiemerie, Chisom, Lugard, Raniel, and my late mother, mummy Margaret Nnadi.

Start The Day Right

Early to bed, early to rise.

Ps. 5:3 "My voice shalt thou hear in the morning, O LORD; in the morning will I direct [my prayer] unto thee, and will look up."

Going to bed early will help you wake up bright and early. Always start your day with a prayer.

(Pray)

God our father, thank you for today, guide my parents, teachers and guide me in all I do.

Respect 1

Always respect your parents.

Ex. 20:12 "Honor (respect, obey, care for) your father and your mother."

As soon as you see mummy and daddy first thing in the morning always say "good morning". The same goes for uncles and aunties.

(Pray)

Dear Lord, please help me to always honour my mother and father.

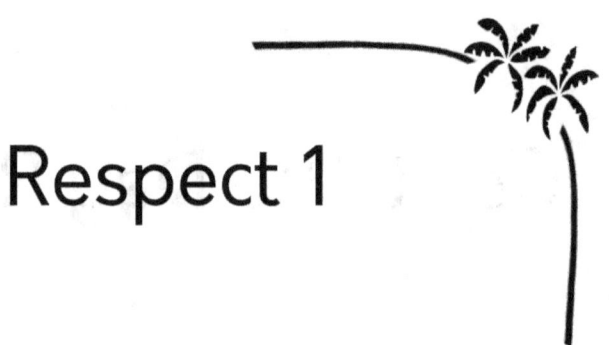

Respect 2

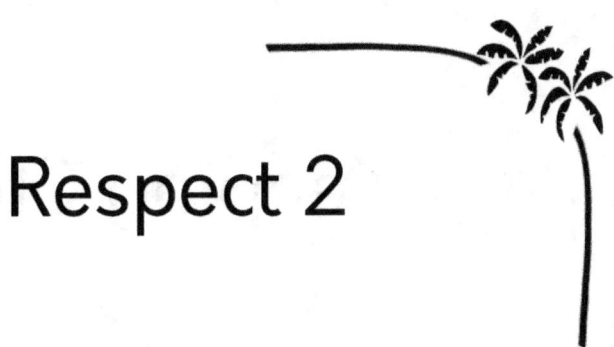

Always respect your elders.

Rom. 13:7 "Render to all their due respect, fear to whom fear, honour to whom honour."

Don't be rude to those older than you, always be respectful.

(Pray)

Dear Lord, please help me to always respect my elders and those in authority.

Keeping Clean 1

Good hygiene means keeping yourself and your environment clean.

Is. 1:16 "Wash yourselves, make yourselves clean."

Always brush your teeth twice a day to be sure you keep tooth cavities and gum disease away.

(Pray)

Dear Lord, help me maintain good personal hygiene.

Keeping Clean 2

Good hygiene means keeping yourself and your environment clean.

Is. 1:16 "Wash yourselves, make yourselves clean."

Always wash your hands with soap and water before meals, and after using the toilet.

(Pray)

Dear Lord, help me maintain good personal hygiene.

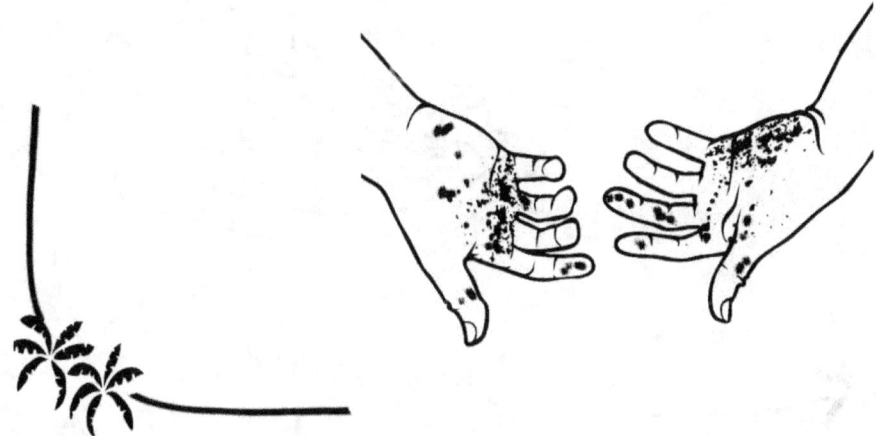

Keeping Clean 3

Good hygiene means keeping yourself and your environment clean.

Is. 1:16 "Wash yourselves, make yourselves clean."

Wash the dishes after you eat and be sure to clean up after you have finished.

(Pray)

Dear Lord, help me keep my home and environment tidy.

Spending time wisely

Reading books is lots of fun, reading is for everyone.

Prov. 3:13-18 "Happy is the person who finds wisdom and the person who gets understanding."

When you come home from school, do your homework. Also remember to read a book everyday because it will make you smart and you will gain a lot of knowledge.

(Pray)

Dear Lord, help me to always make wise decisions so I may walk in excellence.

Honesty

Don't be a talebearer!

Prov.12:22 "The Lord hates people who tell lies, but he is pleased with those who tell the truth."

A talebearer is a person who carries untrue stories. Remember to stay truthful. Don't tell lies, and avoid friends who tell lies against others.

(Pray)

Dear Lord, please help me tell the truth at all times.

Selfishness

Do you help those that are more unfortunate than you?

Prov. 22:9 "Generous people will be blessed, because they share their food with the poor."

Don't look down at people that are poor. Be kind and share your food with those That don't have any.

(Pray)

"Dear Lord, help me not to be selfish, help me to be generous and compassionate".

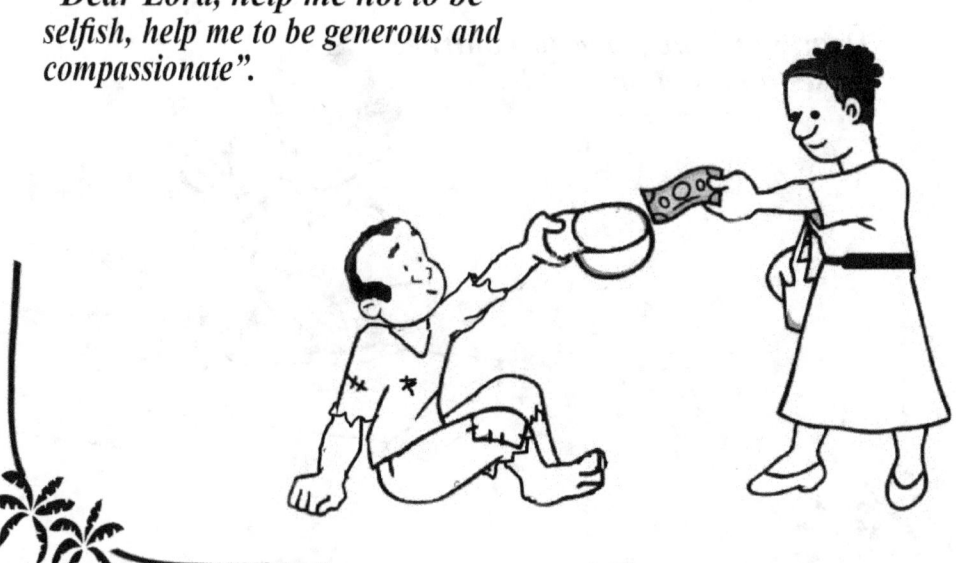

Self Control 1

Don't be greedy.

Prov.23:2 "Control yourself if you have a big appetite."

Do not take food without asking, or take more food than you can eat. When you have an urge to take food ask yourself "Am I hungry?" "Do I really need anymore?"

(Pray)

Dear Lord, help me to control myself and not be greedy.

Self Control 2

Do not steal.

Prov. 15:3 "The Lord sees what happens everywhere; he is watching us, whether we do good or evil."

Sometimes it's tempting to want to take something which is not yours or without asking, however God doesn't like it when we steal. He sees everything.

(Pray)

Dear Lord, help me never to take what is not mine.

Play Safely

Think, look and listen.

Prov. 1:33 "But whoever listens to me will dwell safely, And will be secure, without fear of evil."

Always stay safe; look left and right for moving cars before crossing the road and don't join other children playing in the road.

(Pray)

Dear Lord, please help me to always stay safe and protect me as I go about my day.

Generosity

Give and you will receive.

Deut. 15:10 "You shall give to him freely without begrudging it; because of this the Lord will bless you in all your work and in all you undertake."

Be a giver. Give and do a good deed to someone. There are people who do not have any clothes to wear or food to eat, give what you are able to.

(Pray)

Dear Lord, help me to always give to others without expecting anything back in return.

Control your temper

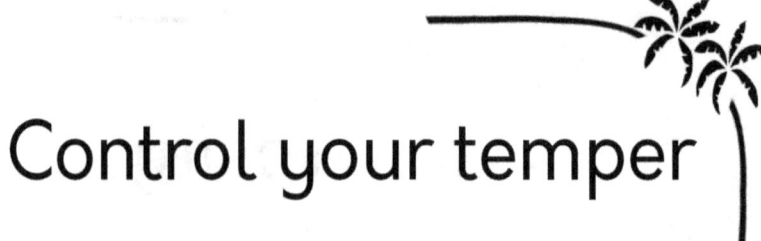

Be slow to anger.

Prov. 16:32 "Controlling your temper is better than being a hero who captures a city."

Do not get in to fights at school or with your siblings at home, instead report to your teacher or parents when someone offends you.

(Pray)

Dear Lord, please help me not to give into anger instead fill my heart with love and patience.

Showing Love

Love your neighbour. Don't discriminate.

Eph. 4:2 "Conduct yourselves with all humility, gentleness, and patience. Accept each other with love."

Show love to others that are different from you, offering a hand to someone who needs help. Also remember to pray for those who offend you.

(Pray)

Dear Lord, please help me to do to others as I want them to do to me.

Worship

Make God number 1.

Mat. 6:33 "But seek first the kingdom of God and his righteousness, and all these things will be added to you."

It is important to go to church and worship God. Before you go to bed it is very important to pray and read your bible.

(Pray)

Dear Lord, please help me to give you first place in my life.

Do good deeds

Do good and good will come to you.

1 Tim. 6:8 "They are to do good, to be rich in good works, to be generous and ready to share."

Aim to do good deeds every day. Help your mummy and daddy around the house. These good deeds will not only please your parents but God too.

(Pray)

Dear Lord, please help me to love others like you do and to do kind things.

Be Prepared

Do not cheat.

***Prov. 11:3** "If you do the right thing, honesty will be your guide. But if you are crooked, you will be trapped by your own dishonesty."*

During an exam do not cheat, instead revise and prepare beforehand. Also remember that cheaters are always caught in the end.

(Pray)

Dear Lord, help me to resist the temptation to cheat during an exam.

Obedience

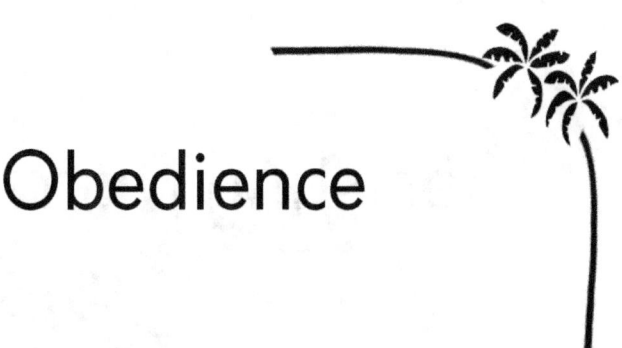

There is beauty in doing your duty.

Prov. 3:1 "My son listen to my instructions."

Obeying instructions keeps us from making mistakes and keeps us out of trouble .

(Pray)

Dear Lord, please give me patience and obedience to obey the words of my parents.

Resisting Distractions

A slow car will not travel far.

Prov. 4:25 "Let your eyes look straight ahead and your sight be focused in front of you."

Ignore your classmates when they are talking to you during a lesson, as they are only distracting you. Remember, when you allow yourself to be distracted, your grades will slip.

(Pray)

Dear Lord, please help me to remain focused at all times so I can excel in my studies.

Be Content

Accept things as they are.

Heb. 13:5 "Your way of life should be free from the love of money, and you should be content with what you have."

There are times when your parents are not able to do or afford certain things. You may wish to be like your friends or neigbours, be happy and enjoy the time you have with them.

(Pray)

Dear Lord, please give me the patience and understanding when things dont go according to plan.

Always Be Thankful

Count your blessings.

Ps. 107:1 *"Give thanks to the Lord, because he is good; his love is eternal."*

Be grateful for every good thing that comes to you no matter how small. Today, count all your blessings and be thankful. Remember to always end your day with a prayer.

(Pray)

Dear Lord, please help me to always be thankful.

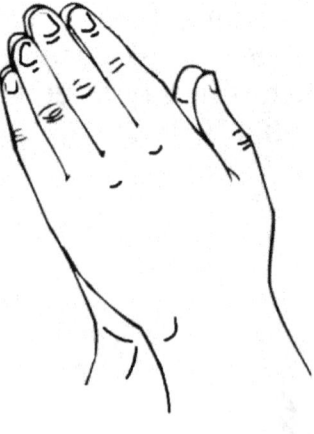

Other books by author

A Rich King And An Old Woman Beggar

The Proud Girl

Contact Author: oluchiabel00@gmail.com

www.ingramcontent.com/pod-product-compliance
Lightning Source LLC
Chambersburg PA
CBHW070343120526
44590CB00017B/2991